50 *Sanity Saving* Tips for Caregivers

You Don't Have to Kill Yourself to Keep Them Alive

Copyright © 2015 Carol Core

All rights reserved. This book or any portion thereof may not be reproduced or used in any manner whatsoever without the express written permission of the publisher except for the use of brief quotations in a book review.

Cover Design and Interior Book Design:
Jane Doe Consulting

Cover Photo: Veer Stock Images, Photographer IKO

Interior Art: Art Explosion

Editing: Amy Guettler, The Perfect Page

Ordering Information:
Quantity sales. Special discounts are available on quantity purchases by organizations, associations and corporations. For details, please contact CarolCARE, LLC:
Tel: (303)780-7347; Fax: (303)398-7010;
www.CarolCARE.net

Printed in the United States of America

First Printing, 2015

ISBN 978-0-9961998-0-3, Softcover

CarolCARE, LLC
www.CarolCARE.net

50 *Sanity Saving* Tips for Caregivers

You Don't Have to Kill Yourself to Keep Them Alive

Carol Core

Introduction

Are you the nonpaid family caregiver of an elderly loved one? I'm betting you are, or you wouldn't have picked up this book.

As a nonpaid family caregiver, you've most likely become exhausted, overwhelmed and perhaps a bit overweight. On a good day, you're seething with resentment and ready to pull out your hair. But I want you to know this: *You are not alone.*

Currently, there are more than 65 million nonpaid family caregivers in the United States, and with the aging of the Baby Boomers, that number is only growing. Approximately 66 percent of family caregivers today are women older than age 50, and more than half of all caregivers also have minor children or grandchildren living with them at home. Clearly, the emotional and physical toll on those who provide care for others is absolutely enormous. It's no wonder you feel overwhelmed, and the potential impact on your health as a caregiver is staggering.

In fact, stress has been shown to impact caregivers' immune systems for as many as three years after their caregiving duties come to an end, which only increases their chances of developing a chronic illness themselves. The psychological effects of caring for a loved one are equally burdensome, as 40 percent to 70 percent of family caregivers experience clinically significant symptoms of depression. In fact, the stress levels can be so extreme it can take as many as 10 years off a family caregiver's life expectancy!

The financial implications of caregiving are also incredible. Did you know that caregivers who give "free" care for their aging, chronically ill or disabled family members or friends provide a combined value of services estimated to be greater than $375 billion a year? That's nearly twice as much as what Americans actually spend on home care and nursing home services combined ($158 billion)! Even worse, just shy of half (47 percent) of all caregivers indicate that an increase in caregiving expenses has caused them to exhaust most or all of their savings. And it doesn't stop there. American businesses lose as much as $34 billion each year due to lost productivity and employees' needs to care for elderly or ill loved ones.

Clearly, caring for your elderly one can take a huge toll on your health, your finances and your life!

At this point you may be wondering why I know so much about caregiving. Am I a geriatric specialist? Am I a prominent researcher, psychologist or the CEO of a large chain of skilled nursing centers? No. I am Carol Core, and I know exactly what your life as a nonpaid family caregiver looks like because for more than 12 years, I was the nonpaid family caregiver for my three favorite "old people" (as I affectionately refer to them) — Mom, Dad and dear Uncle Earl. Now, I'm certainly not suggesting that each of the above-mentioned professionals doesn't have some great information to share; however, unless they were actual caregivers for their own family members, they simply do not know what you and I know. While they undoubtedly possess great knowledge and skills, they've never been in the trenches of day-to-day caregiving.

In fact, depending on how long you have been a caregiver, you've likely come to realize that your family members and friends who aren't in the throes of caregiving have absolutely no understanding of what you go through on a daily basis. As one of my dear friends said, "I am so sorry... Until I became the caregiver for my dad and my grandmother, I realized I had no idea what you were living through all those years."

My life as a caregiver felt like a circus. Performing nothing short of a dizzying juggling act, I worked full time and yet somehow fulfilled my roles as a wife, mother and grandmother, all while managing the care, health, finances and safety of three elderly people.

Over 12 years, I was forced to learn all the complicated ins and outs of in-home care: Medicare versus Medicaid; wills and trusts; powers of attorney (POAs); assisted living and fire safety; long-distance care and Veterans' Benefits; do-not-resuscitate orders (DNRs) and living wills; nursing homes and adult daycare centers; oxygen and medications; food service and feeding; *Depends*; clinical depression and congestive heart failure; crematoriums and funeral homes; and every other conceivable aspect of caring for our elders.

After 12 years of caregiving and another four years working through the effects caregiving had on me, I finally came out of the fog. I leveraged my personal expertise and knowledge to create CarolCARE — a firm dedicated to offering support, empowerment and hope to you, the caregiver. I suppose most people might have pulled their life back together and simply moved on, but I couldn't do that. I just couldn't leave you other caregivers out there on your own, not knowing what lay ahead. Until you've had to live through everything involved with being a family caregiver, you cannot possibly understand the toll it will take on your life. That's why I feel compelled to arm you with information, time-savers and personal stories that can help you not only to survive the perils of eldercare, but also to have a life after caregiving. I want you and the rest of your family to have a quality life characterized by health and happiness. In fact, I am so passionate about this mission that I now speak, coach and consult on the subject of **care for the caregiver**.

Through my own personal experience, I realized that most people never expect to become caregivers, and there simply is no training. It just kind of happens one day — Mom is doing great living on her own and then she takes an unexpected fall. Dad is caring for Mom and they're still living independently when Dad suddenly has a stroke. Grandma still lives in her own home and drives herself everywhere, and then one day she just forgets where she lives. The stories are countless, but as you know all too well, they are real. Caregivers never plan for this, and unfortunately, most of our elderly loved ones don't plan for it either.

Your adventure in eldercare will be challenging, but I can teach you how to save your sanity and navigate through the daunting caregiving landscape. I promise that if you take care of yourself first and follow these sanity-saving tips, there will be life after caregiving.

Special Thanks:

To my darling six and a half year old granddaughter who caught the biggest of typos.

Dedication

This book is dedicated to my dear, sweet Mom, Dad and dear Uncle Earl, who despite endless moments of frustration, pain and overwhelming exhaustion, clearly enriched my life. Indeed, over the course of 12 years, I considered caring for them to be nothing less than a genuine honor and a gift.

This book is also dedicated to my wonderful and brilliant daughter and darling son-in-law, as well as to my precious husband for their years of unbelievable patience and support through my numerous screaming sessions and one too many dinners at the Black-Eyed Pea.

I also dedicate this book to my dear friend Vicki, who, while caring for her mother, was not only my longtime sidekick, but also my weekly support in friendship and laughter over endless plates of Mexican food.

Finally, I dedicate this book to you and the other 65 million nonpaid family caregivers in the U.S., along with the millions of others across the globe who find themselves engaged in some level of family caregiving.

You are the angels on earth. You are beautiful, fearless, kind and brave, and you will stay the course even when you are completely and totally exhausted simply because you know it's the right thing to do. *You are my tribe!*

1. Care for yourself first.

Our mantra and message at CarolCARE is, *"Put your oxygen mask on first before assisting those around you."*

When you fly, why do you think the flight attendants say, "In case of an emergency, secure your own oxygen mask before assisting others"? They say it because if you are not breathing, you certainly can't offer assistance to your child or the elderly relative seated next to you! Well, my friends, the same is true of caregiving. If you aren't breathing and safe, your loved ones won't be either. It is absolutely mandatory that you care for yourself first. It is truly noble that you are so generously giving your time to care for your elderly loved one, but sacrificing yourself to keep your loved one alive isn't helping anyone. I didn't realize this how crucial this rule was until it was almost too late and I nearly killed myself.

Don't let this happen to you!

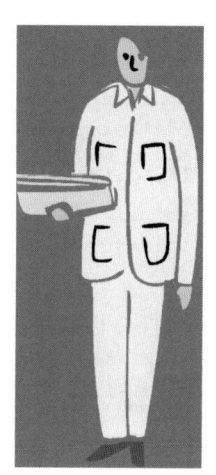

2. Connect directly with your loved one's doctor(s).

Do you need special permission to talk with your elderly relative's doctor(s)? Yes, due to a federal law called the Health Insurance Portability and Accountability Act of 1996 (HIPAA), which established rules for health care providers and plans regarding who can look at and receive an individual's health information, including those closest to us, such as family members and friends.

Knowing exactly what is going on medically with your loved one will make your job as caregiver so much easier. If you've been caregiving for a while, you probably already know that your loved one can grant you access to their medical information by signing a permission form that allows you and his or her doctor to discuss their medical issues in order to determine the best course of care.

Oftentimes you can make contact with your loved one's doctor online or via the phone, saving yourself hours of time and unneeded doctor visits. However, when I teach caregiver workshops, I am always surprised by how many people already in the midst of caregiving have no idea that they can and should be in contact with their loved ones' doctors.

3. Keep a current list of your loved one's medications.

Keep this medication list current (date the list every time you add, change or remove a medication) and keep a copy with you at all times. Also make sure you leave a copy with your loved one in case of an emergency. You never know when your loved one will suffer a fall or a stroke and you'll need to inform emergency personnel of all the meds he or she is taking. Keeping a current medication list posted on the refrigerator will also save time. If you aren't there when emergency personnel are called, they can still reference a current meds list and provide appropriate care for your loved one.

4. Create a boundary around yourself.

I call this the Caregiver Bubble™. This is an imaginary field or boundary that you create around yourself to keep a protective distance between you, your loved one for whom you provide care and your siblings, not to mention their problems, their anger and their guilt trips. As the caregiver, you must protect yourself — from stress, from mental and physical exhaustion, from your loved one's attempts to consume all of your time, etc.

Caregiving is a naturally very emotionally charged activity. Family dynamics often come into play and your loved ones can easily drain you of your life force and drag you into the dance. Your job is to provide care for your loved one, but you must survive the process in order to have a quality of life after caregiving.

5. Work your elderly loved one into your day — not the other way around.

Your elderly loved one usually has all the time in the world to go to the doctor, but you typically do not. So, always schedule your loved one's needs into your schedule and do not let them drag you into theirs! One way to do this is for you to take over the scheduling of their doctor appointments and for you to decide when it works best for you to take them to the store. You are doing a great service by caring for your loved one, and you need to control your life. This alone will help free up some of your valuable time and reduce some of your stress!

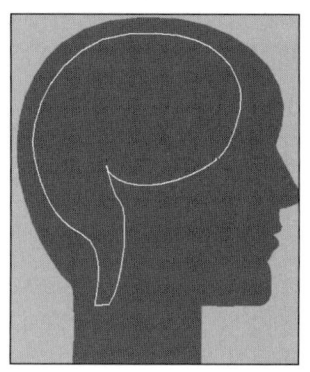

6. Knowledge is power.

The more you know about your options, the process and the available resources, the easier your job as caregiver will be. That's why www.carolCARE.net offers a one-stop shop for all the fundamentals of eldercare as well as great resources and tips to better care for yourself. At CarolCARE, we are constantly working to update information in order to help you quickly research things like Medicare versus Medicaid, Alzheimer's, VA benefits, skilled nursing care versus assisted living, financial planning, end-of-life decisions, how better to care for yourself as caregiver, and hundreds of other eldercare and caregiver-related topics. We also offer links to relevant groups simply because many other people and organizations know more than we do.

Our goal is to put all this information in one easy-to-access location so you can quickly get the information you need without wasting your precious time. We want to save you time to help save your life!

7. Have a plan.

Your role as caregiver just sort of happens one day. Your elderly loved one is doing fine and then falls and breaks a hip, has a car accident or suddenly can't remember where they live. Instantly you become a caregiver. You were already leading a full life, and now you have your loved one's whole life to balance alongside your own. Although this seems like something for which you clearly don't have the time, your life will be a lot less stressful if you step back and develop some sort of plan for the care and safety of your elderly loved one. This may seem like a ridiculous idea in light of the house that's just been dropped on you; however, if you can carve out just a bit of time sooner rather than later, it will make your life easier in the long run. If you have no idea where to start, visit www.carolCARE.net for some helpful hints.

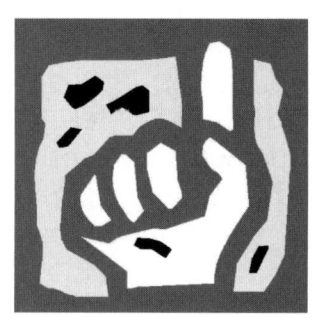

8. One positive thing a day.

The longer you provide care, the higher the possibility that you'll become less positive than you once were. No matter how exhausted you are, before your head hits the pillow at the end of every day, stand in front of the bathroom mirror and tell yourself (out loud) one positive thing that happened that day. Reminding yourself of and recounting this positive event aloud will leave you with a happy thought to sleep on rather than dwelling on the negatives from the nightly news or the frustration of the argument you had with your mother.

In fact, you may even want to create a "happiness jar." What is a happiness jar? It's simply a place to store all of your happy thoughts. In fact, creating a simple happiness jar for depositing and collecting all your cheerful thoughts and memories can lead to years of gratitude and joy.

This idea comes from Elizabeth Gilbert, author of the book *Eat, Pray, Love*. Here's how it works: 1) find or buy a really cool jar; 2) each day, add a little note describing that day's best moment; 3) repeat this process every day; and 4) reap the benefits of being grateful and

happy. Even if you are stressed, overwhelmed and possibly in conflict with the loved one you care for, on the really tough days, you can simply reach into the jar and pull out a happy memory.

Being a caregiver can be overwhelming and sometimes it will be tough to stay upbeat, but remember you are truly making a difference for the positive in the life of your elderly loved one.

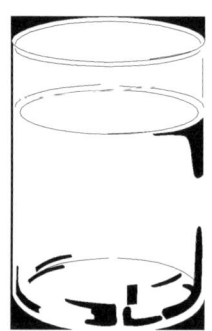

9. Drink more water.

When humans get dehydrated we tend to feel sluggish. Water, not coffee, is the ideal pick-me-up to help you get through the day, as the more hydrated you are, the clearer your thinking. What's more, water also makes you feel more full and less hungry, which can potentially lessen the possibility of weight gain that often accompanies stress.

The human body is made up of two-thirds water, so doesn't it stand to reason that you'll operate more effectively if you keep yourself well-hydrated? The same is true for your elderly loved ones. Older folks typically aren't so good at staying hydrated, but doing so can help improve their digestion, their joint movement and even their mindset.

Remembering to hydrate can be tough, especially when we are so busy. So, buy some sort of large water bottle, fill it up and keep it with you at all times as a reminder. You may want to do the same for your elderly loved ones to encourage them to drink more water, and then keep on hydrating!

10. Keep important documents related to your elderly loved one close at hand.

The longer you provide care and the more involved your loved one's care becomes, the more you may need the following items: power of attorney; a DNR (do not resuscitate) form and a current list of their medications, just to name a few. Make certain you keep copies of these items on or near you at all times. The Caregiver's Pocket Guide and All-In-One Organizer: Your Lifeline to Easy Eldercare (coming soon at www.CarolCARE.com) provides an easy way for you to keep these and other important documents organized and on-hand. It also provides a place to keep important contact numbers and other information related to your loved one's care.

11. Take control of important documents (or at least make copies).

If your loved one has documents that will be important later on, such as a will, a property deed, or life and/or long-term care insurance policies, you not only want to determine where these documents are, but also take control of them if possible.

As humans get older, we sometimes become more paranoid. With this in mind, your elderly loved one may decide to hide one or more of these documents for "safekeeping." Unfortunately, we also become more forgetful as we age, so your loved one may hide certain documents only to forget where they hid them later. I once devoted three weeks to searching for the deed to my parents' home after my father decided he should put it "somewhere safe." *Yikes!*

If you have a good relationship with your loved one and they are comfortable with you taking over the management of their documents, then it should be fairly easy to place this important paperwork in a secure place, like a safety deposit box. However, if your loved is experiencing some issues with paranoia, then I suggest you remove the documents without their knowledge, make copies and return them to the little box under the bed. Sometimes, as caregivers, we have to resort to desperate measures to ensure the safety and well-being of our elderly loved ones.

12. Work with a coach.

Sometimes we are just so close to our own situation and all the family dynamics surrounding it that we can't seem to think straight. The care of your loved one may be so emotionally charged that you and your family members might not even see solutions that could make the situation easier, less time-consuming and ultimately, less stressful for everyone.

This is why working with a coach — a third-party individual who can look at your situation and your family dynamic objectively and serve as a neutral sounding board when no one else will listen — can be so helpful. They can also give you the regular support you need to get through this exhausting process. A coach with specific experience in caregiving and eldercare can provide a valuable set of fresh eyes to look into your life as caregiver and see things you and your family members may not be seeing. At www.carolCARE.net we can help you find a coach or coaching program that best meets your specific needs.

13. Engage all of the players... or at least know where they are on the field.

This tip relates to other family members and the "joy" of your family dynamic as it relates to caregiving. I almost always find that no matter how many siblings there are, more often than not just one person really rises to the surface as the primary family caregiver.

If you are the primary caregiver, you may have siblings or other loved ones who are not doing their share to help you with caring for your elderly loved one. Oftentimes, however, siblings and family members are more than willing to share their opinion about all of the things you aren't doing correctly, but they may not actually be willing to step up to the plate to truly help you. This is where having a plan can really help (refer to Tip No. 7). If you create a care plan that includes these people somewhere, it will make it easier to hold them accountable for taking part in caregiving for your loved one. It will also give them an opportunity to experience, first hand, what you are going through in the day-to-day task of caregiving. They may have a different take on things after they have walked in your shoes for a while.

14. Pace yourself.

There is no way to know how long your job as caregiver will last. Your loved one may live for years, with you at the caregiving helm. Initially you will think you can easily add these extra caregiving tasks into your already busy life, but as time goes on, you will begin to fade. That is when the problems begin: You stop exercising, stop seeing friends, you give up the book club or you stop reading and going to the movies. Altogether, you make these sacrifices because you are doing a great service for your loved one. But take it easy and understand that you have no idea how long this will last. Help them and do what you can, but don't lose sight of your own life and the things that keep you alive and happy while providing care.

15. Remember to laugh!

Somehow, some way, you must find your sense of humor in the midst of the stress-filled job of caregiving. If you don't have a natural sense of humor, watch or listen to people who do! The adage that "laughter is the best medicine" is absolutely true. It is the one thing that got me through 12 years of caregiving for three elderly people. Occasionally, I would just step back and laugh at all of the insanity involved with the job. That moment of letting go actually fortified me with additional strength to get me through another day, week and even years!

I also find that an inflatable rubber chicken or an emergency clown nose can really come in handy for a laugh or two. And who wouldn't laugh at the "Nine Ways to say No" button or the "WTF Slammer" button! This all may seem absolutely ridiculous, but these are desperate times. If it makes you laugh, then your endorphins kick in and you'll feel better, even if it's just for a moment. Turn to the back of this book for links to where you can find chickens, noses and other suggested items of humor, and *keep on smilin'!*

16. Exercise for you.

You simply have to keep moving! Honestly, even if it's just a walk around the block, you are still moving. In your role as caregiver, it's natural that you may begin to feel exhausted and overwhelmed. So on the rare occasion that you do get a few extra minutes to yourself, you'll probably just want to rest, but try to move around instead. If you can't find 20 minutes in the morning to do a quick Zumba tape, just throw on some comfy clothes and a jacket and walk around the neighborhood for 15 minutes (see Tip No. 19, "Schedule some YOU time").

I just couldn't seem to get back into a regular exercise routine, so I started taking this quick little walk every day. Before I knew it, I had lost 10 pounds! If this sounds good to you then just start walking. Honestly, this simple bit of movement has transformed my life! If you want more details about the effects of walking check out the books I recommend at the back of this book.

17. Do not resuscitate.

A DNR form is one of the most important documents you'll want to have when caring for an elderly loved one. With this document, you'll want to make sure that everyone (i.e., family members, physicians, hospitals, emergency personnel, etc.) knows your loved one's wishes and abides by them.

Here is an interesting thing to note about DNRs: You may find that your loved one isn't very agreeable to signing a do-not-resuscitate order, as they may tell you they want to "live at all costs." However, what many people do not realize is that elderly people typically do not resuscitate well. In fact, during Dr. David Davis's 33 years as an emergency room doctor — mostly in hospitals in Maryland and now at Christian Hospital in St. Louis — Dr. Davis estimates he has resuscitated some 600 people. Cardio-pulmonary resuscitation (CPR), he likes to point out, was developed during the Korean War to help wounded soldiers — otherwise healthy young men — stay alive until they reached field hospitals. But performing chest compressions on fragile old people disturbs him.

"It is violent," Dr. Davis said in an interview. "If you don't do it hard enough, you can't move any blood." But even if you do perform the thrusts hard enough, "...you're going to break the ribs and maybe the sternum."

He worries about the few older people he may have saved — especially about whether they will ever recover their strength and functionality after days or weeks in intensive care. "If older people and their families knew all that was involved, the manipulation, the tubes, the drugs and the low chances for a good outcome," maintains Davis, "they'd opt for comfort care instead."

My advice is once you have a DNR, make sure you print copies for everyone. Keep the original in a safe place, and then make a copy for your loved one and for each of your siblings, and definitely post a copy on your loved one's refrigerator.

Why so many copies? Consider this anecdote from my own personal experience. The rehab facility where my dear mother lay in her death bed suggested they did not have a copy of her DNR in her file (even though I had personally given it to them just days before). Without it they could not allow my mother to pass, and would instead be required to attempt resuscitation. What? Yes indeed, it was true!

So our hospice worker raced back to my mother's apartment to retrieve the copy of the DNR off her refrigerator. She promptly delivered it back to the front desk staff at the facility.

With my daughter and me by her side, my dear sweet mother passed peacefully, but only because of darling Mia, our hospice representative who had the wherewithal to recover the copy of Mom's DNR order.

18. Power of attorney versus personal representative.

If you have power of attorney for your loved one, you serve as their representative only while they are alive. If you have medical power of attorney, you can take part in all the decision making regarding medical issues, and if you have financial power of attorney, you have the right to be involved in financial decisions. Depending on the situation and other siblings or family members, being the responsibly party for both your loved one's medical and financial needs can be very helpful and make your job slightly easier. Remember, these documents and your duties as they relate to them are only useful while your loved one is living.

If you are still hoping to manage everything related to your loved one once they have passed, such as funeral arrangements, their estate or their affairs, you need to have been named as executor of their estate and/or their personal representative. These details are generally spelled out in your loved one's will, so a lawyer specializing in estate planning or elder law can be a great help in creating such a will. You can also find a simple will on LegalWiz.com, although I recommend that you seek legal advice when completing this document.

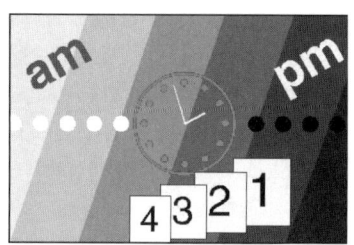

19. Schedule some YOU time in your calendar.

You most likely have some sort of calendar to manage your life, so treat yourself like a client, a business meeting or a friend and schedule a time to get together with you! Schedule at least three, one-hour-long appointments a week for you, with you, and that are all about you. It's incredibly important to make time for you, and you're the only one who can do it. So no matter what happens, don't cancel your appointments with yourself. These appointments are as important to your health and wellbeing as water is to a whale.

20. Doctor appointments become social events?

As your loved one becomes more isolated, they may begin to manifest ailments just so they have a seemingly legitimate reason to schedule a doctor's appointment. Naturally, you will make the appointment and take the time off work to take them, but once you and your loved one are settled into the exam room, you discover there is really nothing medically wrong. Rather, your loved one was simply looking for an opportunity to "visit." When doctor appointments become social events, this is often an indicator that you need to find an activity your loved one can engage in that's easily accessible from their location. There's no use in you wasting gas, time off from work and co-pays just for a social call!

21. Seek support — remember others are also going through this caregiving journey, too.

Find or create a group of other caregivers to get together with for an hour or so each week. This group of people honestly needs to be other caregivers going through the things you are going through... otherwise they will not understand your stress, your frustration and your dilemma. If you live in a small town or you just can't seem to find a group of mutually compassionate people, go to www.Carol-CARE.net. We offer a weekly teleseminar for caregivers that provides resources, support and relief each and every week. Wherever you happen to be, you can simply dial in on your phone and get tips, hear interviews with experts, and feel the strength of endless support from Carol Core and other caregivers who have lived through the journey of caregiving.

The point is that your role as nonpaid family caregiver is very specialized and you need to connect with others who really understand what you're experiencing. If you don't find the right people to support you, you'll feel like a tech support person at a quilting convention. They won't understand what you're going through and honestly they won't understand how to support!

22. You are going to feel guilty.

It doesn't matter how much you do or how much time you spend doing it, what you do for your loved one is never going to feel like enough. Or worse yet, the elderly loved one you provide care for may constantly remind you that they don't think you're doing enough.

Pay close attention to these statements: What you are doing for your elderly loved one is amazing, and you are awesome! All of your time, effort and self-deprivation is beyond incredible! There are literally millions of elderly folks in the U.S. who don't have anyone to help them, and a great many seniors have no one to serve as their advocate apart from certain government programs.

No matter what the level of care you are providing, you have made a conscious decision to help and care for your loved one, and your efforts are to be recognized and commended.

23. Don't lose your own identity in the role of caregiver.

It may become all too common for you to hear the question "How's your mom?" on a daily basis. The longer you are in the role of caregiver, the more apt you are to discover that your friends, family and coworkers can't seem to find much else to talk about with you. They know you are still dealing with your job as caregiver and see you are exhausted, and they're most likely concerned about your health and wellbeing, but they really just don't know what to say or do. So, your entire existence gets lost in that question of "How's your mom?" Your entire identity has been reduced to this one question. Never mind that you're also an award-winning engineer, marathon runner, pastry chef or an accomplished teacher. Unfortunately, the longer you serve as a caregiver, the less people are able to see past that role. Those incredible qualities and talents specific to you, your work and your life can become harder for them to see, so you must take charge.

If you don't want to lose your identity in the

role of caregiver you must direct or redirect certain conversations. It's perfectly acceptable for you to remind them that you are still here and that you still do a wealth of things in your life other than caregiving your elderly loved.

24. Pharmaceutical companies and doctors are not necessarily a caregiver's friend.

Every year, drug manufacturers and the medical industry make billions of dollars trying to keep our society alive and kicking as long as possible. But in their defense, we Americans (and especially the Baby Boomers) have asked them to do this. Boomers account for more than 55 million of the nation's 65 million caregivers, and as a general rule, this generation wants to stay alive as long as possible while also maintaining a quality of life.

In the world of eldercare, however, constantly trying to keep your loved ones alive doesn't necessarily mean they have what can be described as "quality of life." In many cases, the elderly are simply being propped up with massive amounts of medication and ultimately spending their final years managing pills. Then your loved one suddenly needs a caregiver, and then you're spending your time managing those same pills. Additionally, many pills can have side effects that require even more pills, and some medications interact negatively with others, which only causes more problems.

For instance, the father of one of my clients had developed a nonstop, incessant cough. He suffered with it for months. If not for the keen research of a longtime local pharmacist and friend, it might have killed him. As it turned out, the pharmacist finally tracked all of the side effects of the medications the doctors had collectively prescribed and discovered that one of his heart medications, when mixed with another medication, was causing the issue. Within only two days of discontinuing the problem medication, the cough stopped.

Step back from the situation and honestly assess what benefit all of these drugs are bringing to your loved one. Your elderly family member is fortunate to have you as their advocate, so don't be afraid to challenge the doctors or the medications they prescribe.

My darling uncle Earl, a man fearful of making many big decisions though out his life, at 89 years young decided he just didn't want the burden of taking countless pills any longer. At a routine doctor visit he announced his request and after reviewing his list of medications, the doctor agreed to take him off of everything except a pill for prostate, which would keep him from experiencing extreme discomfort.

My uncle was of sound mind when he came to this conclusion, and I was so proud of him for stepping up and making this decision for himself. He lived the last year of his life with less stress and less grief from the encumbrance of pill management.

25. Protect all assets — both your loved one's and your own.

It is never too soon to start talking with your loved one about protecting their assets. The more you can protect, they more money you can set aside for their eldercare. Currently, the average skilled nursing facility costs somewhere between $5,500 and $8,500 a month, so as you can see, even $200,000 in assets is not going to last very long.

You'll also want to preserve your own assets. Quite frankly, it might be nice if you, as the caregiver, got a small reward at the end of your caregiving adventure.

Your elderly loved one may be very private about their finances and their assets, and they may not be willing to discuss this aspect of their lives with you. However, you can explain that this will ultimately assist you to helping and caring for them. It may also be helpful to bring in a reputable financial planner or financial consultant to assist with the details.

26. Who will pay for this care for your elderly loved one.

Well, it's probably your loved one, Medicaid or you. And trust me: You do not want it to be you! As I mentioned in Tip No. 25, the cost of eldercare is staggering. I found that out the hard way when I used my own retirement fund to pay for a portion of my parents' care.

If your elderly loved one has resources, then they typically will pay privately for their care. If you are lucky enough to have had them buy a long-term care policy, it will usually pay for a good portion of their eldercare, depending on the policy. If your loved one is a veteran or the spouse of a veteran, oftentimes some of the expense will be paid through Veterans Benefits. This too depends on the length of service, rank, etc. If your loved one has little or no resources, then they will most likely need to qualify for Medicaid.

You may be wondering what the difference is between Medicare and Medicaid. Medicare is designed to cover regular doctor visits and procedures, and many folks in the U.S. older than age 65 have Medicare. Medicaid, on the other hand, is for long-term care (e.g., assisted living or 24-hour skilled nursing care), but there are certain requirements your loved one must meet in order to apply for and receive Medicaid. You can check out the basics and more Medicaid resources at www.carolCARE.net.

When it comes to Medicaid, the most important things you'll want to note and understand is the required spend-down to $2,000 in total assets and the five-year look-back period when attempting to protect assets. Planning early and long before your loved one needs assisted living or long-term care can insure protection for your loved ones, hard-earned assets. Consult a reputable financial planner or Eldercare lawyer for detailed information and all of the facts, specific to your state.

27. Get a pedicure.

If you have pushed this small treat out of your schedule, add it back in. Oh my gosh, if you have never tried a pedicure, it's time you do. Sitting comfortably for one hour and letting someone rub and care for your feet is one of the most relaxing things you can do for yourself. Our feet are solely responsible for the entire support for our bodies, and until you are sitting in that chair with the feature that massages your back turned on, you have no idea how truly stressed your poor dogs are! This is also a great time to thumb through fashion magazines and trashy gossip rags that you would never ordinarily buy or read. Anything to keep your mind off of your caregiving situation, if only for a little while, is well worth it.

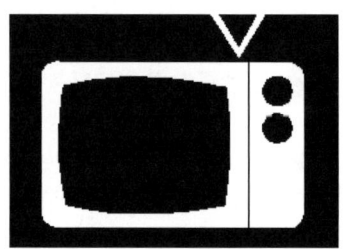

28. Watch one hour of mindless television.

Do not watch the news. Do not watch something political. Do not watch something sad or disturbing. Watch one hour of television that's entertaining — a show that offers something calming or pretty or historically interesting or best of all, something that makes you laugh! Personally, I think Jimmy Fallon is pretty funny, but if you can't stay awake that late, record the show and watch it earlier the next evening. I also happen to like mystery shows — I like to try and figure out "who done it." Not only does this keep me thinking, but more importantly, it also keeps my mind off of my "old people" for an hour.

A nice glass of wine is always a nice addition . . . *red or white will work!*

29. Remember that resentment is natural.

Here's the deal: Your life was already full. You were probably already feeling pretty overwhelmed. And then, out of the clear blue, you suddenly become the caregiver for your elderly loved one, which means your full life just got twice as full. Depending on the level of care you are providing, you now have two sets of bills to pay, possibly two homes to maintain plus two households of laundry to do. On top of that, you've now canceled your trip to the dentist because your loved one needed to go.

Damn right you're resentful, so don't beat yourself up over it! That said, caring for yourself first can help make you a little less resentful.

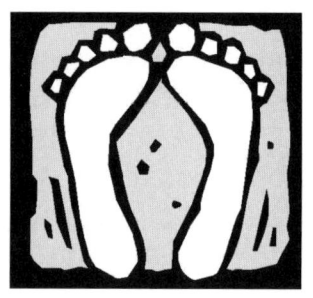

30. Keep your loved one's toenails clipped.

Oh, my goodness, this sounds almost ridiculous and yet so incredibly simple, but it will be one of the most important things you take care of for your elderly loved one.

One of the joys of human aging is that our chemical makeup changes and our toenails tend to get thicker and harder. What's more, elderly folks oftentimes have less mobility. So for an elderly person, that combination often results in the inability to clip their own toenails. If you can't clip your toenails, they grow long and begin to curl under, which means your feet are in constant pain or you have a tough time wearing your shoes. Eventually, this can even lead to problems with in-grown toenails or fungal infections. It's hard to imagine something that seems so insignificant could be the cause of so many problems, but it is! What's the solution? Find a service in your area offering foot care that will clip your loved one's toenails on a regular basis. There are very few people who provide this crucial service, so make sure you get recommendations when you look for someone to take care of this.

The process of successful toenail clipping is really is an art... kind of like cutting your dog's toenails. Most of us don't want to be responsible for that, either, and that's why there are experienced dog groomers. Now, I am not suggesting you take Mom or Dad to the dog groomer (that could be awkward), but do find an experienced toenail/foot care professional and pay them whatever they want. Believe me it is worth it and they deserve it!

31. Get plenty of hugs (mentally and physically).

You are stressed beyond belief and one of the best things you can do is to reach out to other human beings to get a hug… actually, lots of hugs. In fact, Virginia Satir, a respected family therapist, is known for this saying: "We need four hugs a day for survival. We need eight hugs a day for maintenance. We need 12 hugs a day for growth."

"Eight or more hugs a day might seem quite high, but while researching and writing this book I asked my child, 'How many hugs a day do you like?' She said, 'I'm not going to tell you how many I like, but it's way more than eight.' That really made me smile and touched my heart. And, I realized how organic and deep the need for hugs really is."

In fact, research shows that hugging is extremely effective at healing sickness, disease, loneliness, depression, anxiety and stress. Hugging also boosts self-esteem. Those associations of self-worth and tactile sensations from our early years are still imbedded in our nervous system as adults.

The cuddles we received from our mom and dad while growing up remain imprinted at a cellular level, and hugs remind us at a somatic level of that affection. Hugs, therefore, connect us to our ability to self-love.

Hugging also relaxes muscles, balances out the nervous system and releases tension from the body. Hugs can even take away pain; they soothe aches by increasing circulation in the soft tissues. Hugs are very much like meditation and laughter; they teach us to let go and to be present in the moment. They encourage us to flow with the energy of life. Hugs get you out of your circular thinking patterns and connect you with your heart, your feelings and your breath. Find people from whom you can get hugs everywhere you go!

32. Give hugs to your elderly loved one.

As loved ones age they may get a bit grumpy and neglect to bathe as frequently, but when you can, give them hugs. They need to be hugged and touched and loved just as much as you do. They are tired, depressed and isolated. Surprising your loved one with a hug can make a world of difference... in the visit, in their mood and in their day.

Researchers say hugs can instantly boost oxytocin levels, which heals feelings of loneliness, isolation and anger, and holding a hug for an extended period time also lifts one's serotonin levels, thereby elevating their mood and creating happiness. Hugs even strengthen the immune system. This stimulates the thymus gland, which regulates and balances the body's production of white blood cells, which keep you healthy and free from disease. The energy exchanged between two people hugging is an investment in their relationship. It encourages empathy and understanding, and it's synergistic, which means the whole is greater than the sum of its parts: In other words, $1+1 = 3$ or more! This synergy is more likely to result in win-win outcomes.

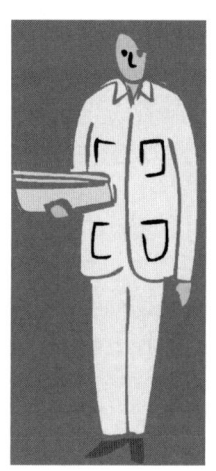

33. Remember your annual exams.

While you're concentrating on the health and wellbeing of other people, things could be festering inside of you. It's kind of like your car — don't wait until the engine seizes up to get your oil changed!

I will again use myself as an example to underscore the importance of this tip. I got so caught up in caring for my three elderly loved ones that I got completely lost in the shuffle. Before becoming a caregiver, I was active and healthy and always watched what I ate. I have scoliosis, which I had always kept in check with a disciplined exercise program. However, as the years went by and the caregiving intensified, I stopped going to my Pilates classes and to my exercise club and ate comfort food instead of healthy foods. With increased stress came weight gain and generally poor health. It ultimately got to the point that I could barely get out of bed in the morning — my body had almost shut down and I had become wrenched with constant pain.

It wasn't until three years after my last elderly

loved one passed that I truly began to eat well again, exercise and regain regular pain-free movement in my body. While in the throes of caregiving I could never have imagined the toll this work was taking on my physical wellbeing. I am a very determined person and plan to be on the planet for a long time for my daughter, husband and precious grandbabies, so I managed to pull myself back out of the hole of poor health.

From the moment you become a family caregiver, be vigilant about protecting your body and your health. Doing so will make you a more productive caregiver so you can give your loved one the best care possible, and after completing your caregiving tasks, you'll bounce back much more quickly.

34. Remember to see your dentist.

Becoming toothless because you haven't cared for your teeth isn't really the best look! And did you know that research shows that poor dental care may be a precursor to Alzheimer's disease?

Researchers from the University of Central Lancashire (UCLan) in the United Kingdom discovered the presence of a bacterium called porphyromonas gingivalis in the brains of dementia patients while they were still alive. This nasty little bug is usually associated with chronic periodontal (gum) disease.

Furthermore, research from New York University (NYU) in 2010 revealed evidence that linked long-term gum inflammation to Alzheimer's disease, finding that gum disease could increase the risk of cognitive dysfunction. (This is a brief excerpt from an article by Honor Whiteman, "Medical News Today," July 31, 2013).

So get regular dental check-ups so you can stay healthy and remember to *smile*!

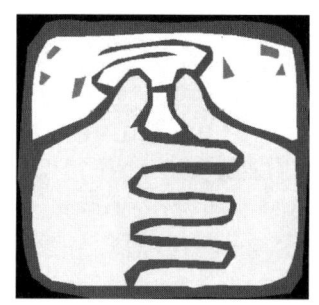

35. Your loved one needs purpose...we all do!

Your loved one will have less health issues and be less depressed and grumpy with you if he or she feels as though they have some purpose. Get creative and find ways to keep them busy! This is vitally important, as author John Cook says, "To matter: to count, to stand for something, to have made some difference that you have lived at all." (The Daily Book of Positive Quotations, Fairfield Press).

Man's Search for Meaning, the 1946 book written by Viktor Frankl chronicling his experiences as a World War II concentration camp prisoner in Auschwitz, centered on the idea of identifying a purpose in life to feel positively about and then immersing oneself in imagining that outcome. According to Frankl, the way a prisoner imagined the future directly affected his longevity, concluding that the meaning of life is found in every moment of living; life never ceases to have meaning, even in the face of suffering and death.

In fact, according to a survey conducted by

the Book-of-the-Month Club and the Library of Congress, *Man's Search for Meaning* belongs to a list of "The ten most influential books in the United States" and has sold more than 10 million copies and has been translated into 24 languages.

At the To Do Institute, they suggest that many Western mental health approaches focus primarily on symptom reduction, as in, "How can we help this person to feel better?" But preoccupation with "feeling better" often distracts us from accomplishing the important purposes of our life. Personally, I agree. Your elderly loved one may not need medication for depression; rather, they may need purpose. So before you rush your loved one to the doctor for medication to combat their depression, look at ways you might get them engaged in worthwhile activities, such as helping school-age kids learn about history, being part of a quilting project or joining the croquet team. These types of activities will likely keep them happy and engaged. Your loved one needs to feel like they still are part of something. They need to feel like they still have something to contribute and they still matter. We all need to feel like we matter!

Purpose also has an impact on our physical health as well. Emerging research shows that the meaning in life predicts better physical health outcomes. A life of greater meaning has been associated with a reduced risk of Alzheimer's disease, reduced risk of heart attack among individuals with coronary heart disease, reduced risk of stroke and increased longevity.

With this in mind, be sure to talk to your loved one about activities in which they might want to get involved — especially those that give them a sense of meaningful purpose. It might help them feel more positive and it will make your job easier as caregiver.

36. Discuss end-of-life issues with your loved one.

This is generally a tough conversation for everyone involved. Your loved one usually doesn't want to discuss their own demise and you may not want to consider the idea of their passing, either. However, it will serve everyone well if you, your loved one and any other siblings or family members can get past these fears and actually discuss their wishes, their finances, etc. With this information you can actually plan ahead; allowing your loved to have a hand in some of the decision making. This will give you all the opportunity to make good, informed decisions so you aren't trying to make difficult choices in the midst of your grief.

One wonderful tool to guide this discussion is called **Five Wishes**. Five Wishes was introduced in 1997 and originally distributed with support from a grant by the Robert Wood Johnson Foundation, the nation's largest philanthropic foundation devoted exclusively to health and health care.

Five Wishes lets your family and doctors know:

1. Who you want to make health care decisions for you when you can't make them.

2. The kind of medical treatment you do or don't want.

3. How comfortable you want to be.

4. How you want people to treat you.

5. What you want your loved ones to know.

Five Wishes is changing the way America talks about and plans for care at the end of life.

More than 18 million copies of Five Wishes are in circulation across the nation, distributed by more than 35,000 organizations. Five Wishes meets legal requirements in 42 states, is useful in all 50, and can be used in any part of the world as both a helpful guide and a documentation of your wishes.

With assistance from the United Health Foundation, Five Wishes is now available in 26 languages. Get your copy of Five Wishes at www.agingwithdignity.org.

37. Pick your battles.

If your loved one is dealing with issues of memory loss, you will often find yourself in conversations in which they are determined not to be wrong about a date, fact or location. They may become fairly adamant about these things in an effort to save face as they realize they really are forgetting things. So pick your battles. You can save yourself time and energy if you don't get caught up in mindless facts. No one really cares if you went to the store on Tuesday or Thursday. If you only correct them when the facts are really important, your time with your loved one will go more smoothly and be more enjoyable for both of you.

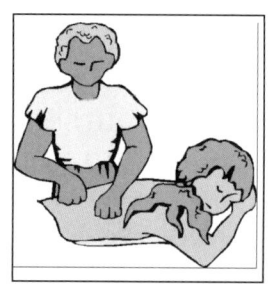

38. Get a monthly massage.

Our bodies are a representation of what is going on in our lives. That is why stress, lack of sleep, lack of movement and dehydration can often result in health problems or weight gain. Find a good massage therapist and schedule a monthly massage. Massage releases tension and toxins from your body that if left to fester, can actually create health issues for you. Now, a monthly massage won't alleviate all of your stress and frustration, but it will keep things from building up and also give you time to yourself to unwind and relax.

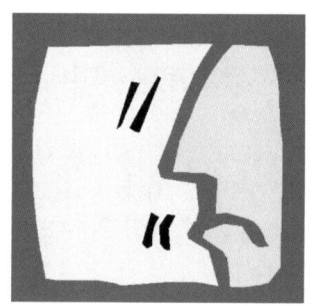

39. Having your elderly loved one live with you may not be the answer.

It all might sound like a nice idea; however, if you are not used to having another person in your home or your home is already the center of plenty of hustle and bustle, adding an elderly person to that equation most likely won't be great for them and it probably won't be good for you. It's a lofty goal that may work in certain situations, but I have seen many a family crumble trying to manage the increased needs of their elderly loved one effectively while still maintaining the rest of the family's sanity.

If you can, keep your elderly loved one in their own home as long as possible. This is the place they are most familiar with and generally, where they'll also be the least confused. If your loved one must be moved to an assisting living or skilled nursing facility, do your homework. Don't just choose a location because you like it. Choose a place that fits the personality of your loved one and will best support them. For more details and ideas on how to choose the right assisted living or skilled nursing facility for your loved one, visit www.carolCARE.net.

40. Connecting with a loved one suffering from memory loss.

If your elderly loved one is experiencing dementia or has been diagnosed with Alzheimer's, your efforts as a caregiver will become even more complex. Now, you (or one of your siblings) may be someone who feels an overwhelming need to be a complete and total realist. You decided Santa wasn't real at the age of four, and you don't believe in the Easter Bunny, fairies or the Loch Ness Monster. But now you have a loved one who is living in and thinking about another reality. Just because it isn't your reality doesn't mean it isn't real — it's real to them!

As my father's Alzheimer's worsened, his reality was often that of the farm, in South Dakota, where he lived as a teen. Some of our best visits were discussions about the crops they might ready for harvest, the farm hands, riding the old tractor and the dance his uncle would host in the barn on Saturday night.

Your visits can be calm and happy if you find out what their reality is that day and then talk to them about that.

41. All in-home care is not created equal.

Sometimes in-home care is your only option. Just understand that it is very costly and you never really know who will be spending time with your loved one, so check out the company thoroughly. Get recommendations. Check with the Better Business Bureau. Has this organization performed background checks on all of its paid in-home caregivers? If so, do they do background checks just for the state in which you live, or do they check with all 50 states? Remember, a caregiver can have a criminal record in another state but their background check in your state can come up clear. A good resource for identifying in-home care companies is the Senior Blue Book. You can get a free copy for your area at their website: www.SeniorBlueBook.com.

42. Call a friend and *don't* talk about your loved one.

Find 30 minutes in your schedule, call a friend and do not talk about your caregiving or your loved one, even if your friend asks. Just say that everything is the same and the reason you called was to catch up with what they are doing and not to talk about your caregiving. They will be thrilled and will probably talk your ear off about some simple thing they are doing or some guy they are dating, but it doesn't matter. You are having a conversation with another human being that isn't your loved one. This conversation isn't about laundry, oxygen, doctor's appointments or *Depends*! This is just a little chat between two friends — connecting, catching up and ultimately enjoying a wonderful exchange.

43. Use hospice to get a break from caregiving.

Working with your loved one's doctor to sign them up for hospice care doesn't mean they are dying tomorrow. It does, however, mean they have enough medical issues going on that their physician feels they could benefit from the extra care. After all, it could actually be two or more years before they pass. But in the meantime, getting your loved one into a hospice program means they will get regular, weekly visits from kind, gentle souls whose only job is to do nice things for your loved one and make them feel comfortable. It's a win-win: Your loved one gets an extra social call with a loving person and you may get one day off from your caregiving duties.

Hospice care is covered under Medicare, Medicaid, most private insurance plans, HMOs and other managed care organizations. Among its major responsibilities, an interdisciplinary hospice team usually provides the following services:

- Coaching the family on how to care for the patient

- Managing the patient's pain and symptoms

- Providing needed drugs, medical supplies and equipment

- Making short-term in-patient care available when pain or symptoms become too difficult to manage at home, **or the caregiver needs respite time**

- Delivering special services such as speech and physical therapy if needed

- Assisting the patient with the emotional, psychosocial and spiritual aspects of dying

- Providing bereavement care and counseling to surviving family and friends

For nearly two years, both Mom and Uncle Earl got to experience the sweet tenderness and care of those extra weekly visits from some of the kindest and most gracious people on the planet. In my opinion, hospice wasn't tied to my loved ones' demise — it was a blessing that brought them comfort, empowerment and light, long before they passed.

44. Last-minute travel deals can make for a great escape from caregiving.

Almost every travel site out there (e.g., Travelocity, Expedia, Orbitz, etc.) has a tab called Last-Minute Deals. In an effort to save yourself and your sanity, you'll occasionally want to go on the Internet, pull up one of these sites and click on that tab. When you click this tab, you will find some incredible package deals for getaways — deals that are perfect for the person who can drop everything and go now. I know, you don't think you can do this. But if you refer to Tip No. 43 and use hospice to watch your loved one through respite care or you ask a friend or family member to care for your loved one for a few days, you can actually go! So go... go NOW!

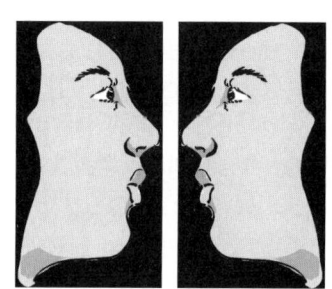

45. "The Mirror Image™"

There is no doubt that your job as a nonpaid family caregiver is a tough one. You never really planned on any of this, but then one day your elderly loved one is in need of assistance and suddenly you are a caregiver. You already had a full life, and now, with all of the things you need to do for your loved one, your life is twice as full. You're tired, you're overwhelmed and you frequently reach your breaking point. It's unbearable for you, but what do you think it's like for them?

Your elderly loved one had their own full, independent life. If they needed a couple of things, they just hopped in the car. They managed their own lives and paid their own bills. Their visits to their doctor were very private, and they certainly could take a bath by themselves and manage their own hygiene. What about now? Now you are doing a lot of these jobs for them and they have lost a great deal of their independence. Maybe they've even had to leave the home they loved so much.

Consider these aspects of the caregiving dynamic:

- They feel isolated.

- This causes them to feel angry and resentful.

- This eventually makes them feel depressed.

- They can't do as much and don't feel like they have any purpose in life, so they focus on tiny details that don't really matter.

Oddly enough, the longer you are the caregiver of your elderly loved one, the more you begin to experience similar feelings.

- You feel isolated because you have had to give up so many of your activities to care for your loved one.

- You too feel angry and resentful.

- You often feel depressed about the situation.

- You find yourself distracted with silly, insignificant details because those seem easier to deal with than the bigger issues at hand!

I call this interesting phenomenon between you and your elderly loved one the Mirror Image™.

If you stop for a moment and realize that you and your loved one are experiencing many of the same feelings, it may help you find a little more compassion in your role as caregiver. It may also be an interesting conversation to have with your loved one, as they might not understand what you are going through.

46. Doing chores for a loved one is not a "visit."

Depending on the depth of your caregiving, you might be with your loved one every day for an hour or maybe more. You stop by, you do their laundry, you prepare their food for the week, you set up their medication and you make certain their oxygen is working properly. You have it down to a science, but they can't understand why you aren't staying to "visit." All of this activity takes a huge chunk out of your daily routine, but in the mind of your loved one, you didn't stay to "visit." You can alleviate some of their frustration by scheduling a certain day of the week for your "visit." You might bring in dinner to share or maybe plan to watch a particular television show together they enjoy. My mother, for instance, loved it when we planned an evening and watched "Dancing with the Stars."

47. After a loved one passes, it still won't be over.

Once your elderly loved one has passed, you will find there is still so much to take care of. You may be inclined to race through everything so you can just be done and get past this chapter of your life, but give yourself time. Give your loved one the sendoff they deserve. Make sure other loved ones get to say their own good-byes as well.

If you feel as though you just can't go through their things right now, then just pack them up; put them in your basement, garage, or a storage unit and then stop. Take care of yourself. Give yourself time to grieve. Those boxes you packed and all of the other stuff won't be going anywhere — they'll be waiting for you when you are emotionally ready to deal with them. Remember, take good care of yourself first!

48. Schedule something just for YOU.

Maybe you love art and a fabulous Matisse exhibit is coming to the local art museum. Perhaps there's a certain activity or a concert that has piqued your interest. Maybe it's just a trip to the zoo where you can eat an ice cream cone and enjoy the fresh air. Even if you can't find someone to go with you, get dressed up and go by yourself; it's better to get out on your own than not to go at all.

Many cities have a free university program that offers tons of interesting courses on a variety of subjects for a very nominal fee. Through all my years of caregiving, I found a way to take at least one class every couple of months. The classes were generally only two or three hours long, but they became a wonderful opportunity to get away, be with interesting people, learn something new and made me feel fulfilled. Years later, I now teach classes at Colorado Free University, and students always tell me how much they appreciate the chance to come to the class and get away for a few hours.

49. Say "yes" to offers for help.

Throughout your efforts as a caregiver, you may be lucky enough to have friends or family members offer to help. As caregivers we are notorious for saying, "Oh thanks so much, but we're fine." **We are not fine! We are overwhelmed, ready to jump off a cliff!** In your heart of hearts you understand that, but by declining help you're just trying to be nice and not burden anyone else with your caregiving crisis. So say "yes" for a change! It doesn't mean you will continually call on them, but let them help you — even if it's only once. I didn't take my own advice and nearly killed myself attempting to be noble.

50. Take yourself to brunch.

Pick a pleasant restaurant on a quiet street with a lovely menu and take yourself to brunch Saturday, Sunday or even sometime in the middle of the week. If you drink, treat yourself to a mimosa or a Bloody Mary. Eat slowly, savor the flavors of the food and just pamper yourself. Do not worry about the calories — you have earned every single one of them! On your way home, stop and buy yourself a bouquet of flowers. Remember to take good care of the person who is taking care of everyone else!

So, dear caregiver, here we are at the end of this list. There is so much more to share, but this is enough to absorb for now. I hope you have found these tips to be informative and enlightening. I hope that for your sake you will apply some of them to your role as caregiver and that you now know you are not alone.

I have many more personal stories to share and resources to offer, so please stop by my website, www.CarolCARE.net any time. Here you will find weekly teleseminar for support, along with family consultation and planning and one-on-one caregiver coaching. At Carol-CARE, **we are here to help you!** I want you to use my years of experience, stories, advice and resources to arm yourself on the battlefield of caregiving.

It may not feel like it now, but you will make it through this. You are doing the right and honorable thing for your elderly loved one, and you will not only make it through this struggle, but you'll also be labeled as one of the angels on earth. You will be forever blessed for your good work.

As a fellow caregiver I send you energy, wisdom and strength, and the biggest and longest of hugs for the incredible work you are doing and will continue to do in your caregiving quest. Know that you are honored, recognized and loved for your noble sacrifice.

My goal and my passion is that your loved ones are safe and get the quality care they need, and that YOU stay healthy and have a quality of life after caregiving.

Take good care of YOU!

Carol Core
President and Founder, CarolCARE
www.CarolCARE.net

Disclaimer

The information contained in this book and on the CarolCARE website is for general information purposes only. The information is provided by CarolCARE and while we endeavor to keep the information up-to-date and correct, we make no representations or warranties of any kind, express or implied, about the completeness, accuracy, reliability, suitability or availability with respect to the website or the information, products, services, or related graphics contained on the website for any purpose. Any reliance you place on such information is therefore strictly at your own risk.

In no event will we be liable for any loss or damage including without limitation, indirect or consequential loss or damage in connection with, the use of this book or use of content contained on the website.

Referenced in this book and through the website you are able to link to other websites which are not under the control of CarolCARE. We have no control over the nature, content and availability of those sites. The inclusion of any links does not necessarily imply a recommendation or endorse the views expressed within them.

Every effort is made to keep the website up and running smoothly. However, CarolCARE takes no responsibility for, and will not be liable for, the website being temporarily unavailable due to technical issues beyond our control.

In addition, Carol Core refers to herself as an Eldercare Expert due to 13 years of personal experience in the care, protection and financial management of her three elderly loved ones. Carol Core and her books, materials and programs offer suggestions, resources and advice to caregivers and their loved ones in an effort to offer resources, relief and hope to caregivers and their loved ones. Information is based on Core's personal experiences as a caregiver as well as research she has done. Core is certified in mediation and conflict resolution, however Core is not a medical doctor, a psychologist, a lawyer or a certified financial planner and does not claim to have credentials related to any of the aforementioned professions. Please consult your own trusted professionals in these areas for specific information, advice and expertise.

References:

Caregiver Statistics:

65.7 million caregivers make up 29% of the U.S. adult population providing care to someone who is ill, disabled or aged. [The National Alliance for Caregiving and AARP (2009), Caregiving in the U.S. National Alliance for Caregiving. Washington, DC.] - Updated: November 2012

43.5 million of adult family caregivers care for someone 50+ years of age and 14.9 million care for someone who has Alzheimer's disease or other dementia. [Alzheimer's Association, 2011 Alzheimer's Disease Facts and Figures, Alzheimer's and Dementia, Vol.7, Issue 2.] - Updated: November 2012

Caregiver services were valued at $450 billion per year in 2009- up from $375 billion in year 2007. [Valuing the Invaluable: 2011 Update, The Economic Value of Family Caregiving. AARP Public Policy Institute.] - Updated: November 2012

More women than men are caregivers: an estimated 66% of caregivers are female. One-third (34%) take care of two or more people, and the average age of a female caregiver is 48.0. [The National Alliance for Caregiving and AARP (2009), Caregiving in the U.S. National Alliance for Caregiving. Washington, DC.] - Updated: November 2012

The cost of informal caregiving in terms of lost productivity to U.S. businesses is $17.1 to $33 billion annually. Costs reflect absenteeism ($5.1 billion), shifts from full-time to part-time work ($4.8 billion), replacing employees ($6.6 billion), and workday adjustments ($6.3 billion). [MetLife Study of Working Caregivers and Employer Health Costs: National Alliance for Caregiving. 2010] - Updated: November 2012

Caring for persons with dementia is reported to impact a person's immune system for up to 3 years after their caregiving experience ends, thus increasing their chances of developing a chronic illness themselves. [The National Alliance for Caregiving and AARP (2009), Caregiving in the U.S: National Alliance for Caregiving. Washington, D.C.] - Updated: November 2012

40% to 70% of family caregivers have clinically significant symptoms of depression with about a quarter to half of these caregivers meeting the diagnostic criteria for major depression. [Zarit, S. (2006) Assessment of Family Caregivers: A Research Perspective in Family Caregiver Alliance (Eds.), Caregiver Assessment: Voices and Views from the Field. Report from a National Consensus Development Conference (Vol. II) (pp. 12-37). San Francisco: Family Caregiver Alliance.] - Updated: November 2012

"Caregiver Syndrome: Reality for Many Caregivers Dealing with Dementia," quoting Dr. Jean Posner,

(Dr. Jean Posner, Baltimore neurologist coined the term "Caregiver Syndrome" in 2007). Clarksvilleonline.com, August 23, 2007, 10:53 AM, online

TIP #2
HIPAA - is the federal Health Insurance Portability and Accountability Act of 1996. The primary goal of the law is to make it easier for people to keep health insurance, protect the confidentiality and security of healthcare information and help the healthcare industry control administrative costs. For more information visit www.hhs.gov

TIP #8
Gilbert, Elizabeth. Eat, Pray, Love, New York: Viking Penguin, a member of Penguin Group, 2006. Print.

Gilbert, Elizabeth. "Happiness Jar." Facebook. Re-posted 2013. Online.

TIP #9
WaterCoolersDirect.com. "The Benefits of Drinking Water." www.MindBodyGreen.com. August 30, 2012, 4:00 p.m. EDT. Article/Presentation. Online.

TIP #10
Core, Carol A. The Caregiver's Pocket Guide and All-in-One Organizer: Your Lifeline to Easy Eldercare, Coming May, 2015

TIP #15
Laughter inducing Chickens, Noses, Buttons, etc.

    Inflatable Chicken – www.Amazon.com
    (Gag Toys and Practical Jokes)

    Nine Ways to Say "NO" Button –
    www.Amazon.com (The NO Button is a handy
    button that says "NO" in 10 Different Variations

    Emergency Clown Nose –
    www.uncommongoods.com

    The WHF Slammer Button –
    www.officeplayground.com

TIP #16
Books on Walking:

Roberts, Katy. Skinny Walking: Walk The Weight Off In 6 Weeks Without Dieting And Even Eat Your Favorite Foods! Copyright Katy Roberts. 2014. Kindle Edition

Mayfore, Jo. Walking for Weight Loss - How to Lose Weight and Burn Fat Just by Walking! Copyright Jo Mayfore. 2014. Kindle Edition.

Jill, Jodi. Successful Secrets to Get Fit Using the 10,000 Steps Exercise Workout: Perfect for Busy Professionals, Moms & Women on Diets. Palolo Papayrus. 2004. Kindle Edition.

Exercises Programs:
Zumba, 20 minutes workout – www.Zumba.com, "Dance fitness that is fun, energetic, and it doesn't feel like work."

TIP #17
DNR – Do Not Resuscitate:
> Visit www.tidyform.com – Each state has their own form. This site offers forms specific to your state or the state where your loved one resides.

Span, Paula. More on CPR for the Elderly. The New York Times. August 10, 2012, 12:52 pm. Print/Online.

Span, Paula. When the Time Comes: Families With Aging Parents Share Their Struggles and Solutions. Paula Span. 2009. Print.

TIP #18
Power of Attorney –
> Visit www.powerofattorney.com - Power of Attorney, Medical, Durable and General - This site offers FREE downloadable forms specific to your state or the state where your loved one resides.

TIP #26
Medicaid Home site - www.medicaid.gov

TIPS #31 & 32
Marcus Julian Felicetti, Yoga Therapist quoting Virginia Satir, Family Therapist. "Hug Therapy." www.MindBodyGreen.com. August 10, 2012, 3:52 pm EDT, Online.

Virginia Satir, Family Therapist, for more information visit www.satirglobal.org

Richardson, Josh. "The Physiological Benefits of Hugging." www.signofthetimes.com, Prevent Disease. Thursday, January 22, 2015, 16:28 CET. Online.

TIP #34
Whiteman, Honor. Alzheimer's Disease Linked to Poor Dental Health. Medical News Today. July 31, 2013, 5:00 am EDT. Online.

TIP #35
Frankl, Viktor. Man's Search for Meaning. First published in 1946 under the title *Ein Psychologerlebt das Konzentrationslager.* This translation first published by Beacon Press in 1959. Copy right 1959, 1962, 1984 Viktor Frankl. New York. Simon and Schuster, Inc., Touchstone Edition (reprinted by arrangement with Beacon Press). 1984.

Picone, Linda. The Daily Book of Positive Quotations. Quotation by John Cook. Minneapolis, Minnesota, Fairview Press a division of Fariview Health Services. 2008.

Baggini, Julian. What's It All About: Philosophy and the Meaning of Life. New York. Oxford University press, Inc. 2004

The To Do Institute –www.todoinstitute.org/purpose. Natural alternatives for mental wellness

TIP #36
Five Wishes, The Robert Wood Johnson Foundation, with assistance from the United Health Foundation Five Wishes forms can be obtained online at Aging with Dignity - www.AgingWithDignity.org

TIP #41
Senior Blue Book – www.SeniorBlueBook.com

TIP #43
The National Hospice and Palliative Care Organization   www.Nhpco.org

TIP #44
Travel Sites, for last-minute travel opportunities:
www.bookings.com
www.kayak.com
www.expedia.com
www.orbitz.com
www.travelocity.com
www.priceline.com

Additional Organizations referenced in this book

The National Alliance for Caregiving –
www.caregiving.org

AARP (American Association of Retired Persons) –
www.aarp.org

National Alzheimer's Association - www.alz.org

National Council on Aging - www.ncoa.org

Carol Core would love to speak to your organization, association or conference

Carol Core is passionate about caring for caregivers!

She is a speaker, author, humorist and President and Founder of CarolCARE, an organization created to offer resources, guidance and support non-paid family caregivers, primarily of the elderly.

Core knows caregiving because for more than 12 years she was the non-paid family caregiver for her three favorite elderly loved ones—Mom, Dad and dear Uncle Earl. Over the years, Carol was forced to learn all the complicated ins and outs of every conceivable aspect of caring for our elders.

Core is compelled to arm caregivers everywhere with information, time-savers and personal stories that can help them not only to survive the perils of eldercare, but also to have a life after caregiving.

Carol Core is certified in mediation and conflict resolution and has nearly 30 years of professional experience in the areas of real estate and marketing. She was a former publisher and corporate marketing VP.

Some Suggested Talks and Workshops Include:

◆The Witch Wasn't Wicked, she was a Non-paid Family Caregiver

◆Mom has Dementia and I'm Losing My Mind: Twelve Years a Caregiver

- Businesses: Care for the Caregivers and Takes Care of Your Bottom Line.

- Planning for Your Future: Don't Outlive Your Money or Your Caregiver.

- Caregivers: Your Health, Your Identiy and Your Life Matter, too.

- Parenting Your Parents: The the Dance and Dynamics of Family Caregiving

- The Most Important Legal Documents You'll Need as a Caregiver and Why

- How to Effectively Connect With Your Loved One Who has Memory Loss

For more information or to schedule Carol Core, please call CarolCARE, LLC at 303-780-7347 or visit our website at www.CarolCARE.net/ speaking.

Here is what people say about Carol Core:

Attendees knew she had walked in their shoes.
They all loved her talk and wanted more.
—Sarah, Denver Post, Amazing Aging Expo

Carol gets rave reviews everytime she holds a class.
—Laura, Colorado Free University

Excellent speaker. Great sense of humor.
Laughed while we learned!
—Aline

Great to have a speaker with so much personal knowledge. I loved all of the real-life stories.
—Robert